7/15

eye-POPPING
CGI

COMPUTER-GENERATED
SPECIAL EFFECTS

BY DANIELLE S. HAMMELEF

Content Consultant:
Mira LaCous
President
Hollywood Pyrotechnics, Inc.

Reading Consultant:
Barbara J. Fox
Professor Emerita
North Carolina State University

Blazers Books are published by Capstone Press,
1710 Roe Crest Drive, North Mankato, Minnesota 56003
www.capstonepub.com

Library of Congress Cataloging-in-Publication Data
Hammelef, Danielle S.
Eye-popping CGI : computer-generated special effects / by Danielle S Hammelef.
      pages cm. — (Blazers books. Awesome special effects)
Summary: "Explains how computer-generated special effects are used in
movies"—Provided by publisher.
Audience: Age 8-14.
Audience: Grades 4 to 6
Includes bibliographical references and index.
ISBN 978-1-4914-2001-0 (library binding)
ISBN 978-1-4914-2178-9 (eBook PDF)
1. Cinematography—Special effects—Juvenile literature. 2. Digital
cinematography—Juvenile literature. 3. Computer animation—Juvenile literature.
4. Three-dimensional imaging—Juvenile literature. I. Title. II. Title: Eye-popping
computer generated image.
TR897.7.H3635 2015
777.7—dc23   2014034098

Editorial Credits
Brenda Haugen, editor; Aruna Rangarajan, designer; Jo Miller, media researcher;
Tori Abraham, production specialist

Photo Credits
Alamy: AF Archive, 21, Franz Pagot, 5, JHP Attractions, 15, LUCASFILM
PARAMOUNT PICTURES/Ronald Grant Archive, 13, 25, Moviestore Collection
Ltd, 11, 23; Photoshot: Cultura/Image Source, cover; Rex USA: MediaPunch Inc,
19; Shutterstock: Kzenon, 4 (inset), Mayskyphoto, 8, SuperStock: Cusp, 7; The
Kobal Collection: Sad Flutes, 29, TF1 Films Productions, 16-17, United Artists,
26-27

Design Elements
Shutterstock: Canicula, donatas1205, escova, freelanceartist, ilolab, Janaka
Dharmasena, Matusciac Alexandru, NikolayPetrovich,
Petr Vaclavek, Ron Dale

Printed in the United States of America in
Stevens Point, Wisconsin
092014   008479WZS15

TABLE OF CONTENTS

REAL TOOLS FOR WILD WORLDS

Monsters eat at restaurants. People become dogs. Amazing worlds are brought to life. How does this all seem so real in movies? Much of the time, you're seeing special effects that moviemakers created on computers.

special effect—a misleading image created for movies by using makeup, special props, camera systems, computer graphics, and other methods

BUILDING ANIMATED CHARACTERS

Amazing animated 3-D characters come to life in movies. Artists create these characters from computer models.

animate—to make something appear to move

3-D—having three dimensions: length, width, and depth

model—something that is made to look like a person, animal, or object

FACT

It can take up to five years to make a movie using characters created on a computer.

Artists mark the characters with hundreds of **controls**. They can make characters smile or stick out their tongues by choosing different control points.

control—a spot marked on an animated character where it can move

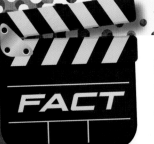

FACT

In the 2013 movie *Monsters University*, Sulley's coat has 5,500,000 moving hairs that are controlled by a computer.

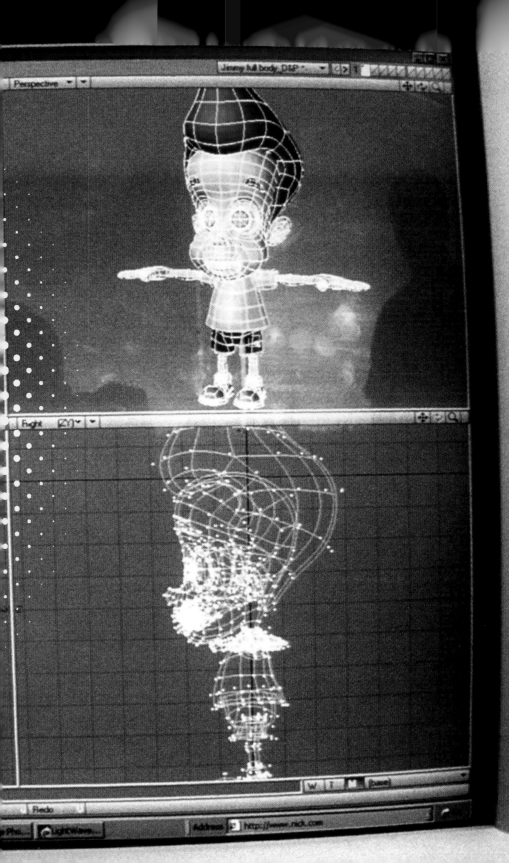

Most movies flash 24 frames per second. A 90-minute movie needs 129,600 frames!

FACT

To show a character's arms rising above its head, an artist first makes a **frame** showing the arms lowered. Then the artist draws a frame with the arms raised. A computer draws the frames in-between to show the character's arms rising in tiny steps.

frame—one drawing or picture in a movie

CHANGING BEFORE YOUR EYES

Computers turn actors into different creatures. To do this, an artist uses a picture of the actor and a picture of the creature. The artist matches the eyes, ears, and chins on both pictures. A computer combines the features.

FACT

A bird became a goat, an ostrich, and then a tortoise in the 1988 movie *Willow*. The tortoise later changed into a tiger and finally, a woman.

Artists also turn actors into **cyborgs**. Artists put blue makeup on parts of actors' bodies. The actors perform in front of blue screens. Computers trade the blue areas on the actors' bodies with robot pieces.

cyborg—a human with robotic parts

MAKING ANYTHING POSSIBLE

Characters fly high in the sky or explore alien worlds. Moviemakers film these scenes with actors in front of blue or green screens. Artists use computers to add background scenery.

green screen >>>

Some characters are missing arms or other body parts. Actors are painted with blue or green makeup or wear blue or green clothing. When actors stand in front of a blue or green screen, the blue or green body parts seem to disappear on film.

FACT

Movie star Chevy Chase wore blue bodysuits under his costumes in the 1992 movie *Memoirs of an Invisible Man*. Chase seemed to disappear, but his clothes could still be seen.

THE BIG FREEZE

Freezing an actor in midair takes many cameras. The cameras are arranged like train cars along tracks. At **freeze-action** moments, computers join pictures taken from all the cameras in track order.

freeze-action—stopped while in motion

FACT

The 1999 movie *The Matrix* used more than 100 cameras to make actors freeze in place.

PLAYING TRICKS ON YOUR EYES

How do people seem to travel in spacecrafts? Directors use computer-guided cameras to film spacecraft models. They use the same camera movements to film the actors. Computers match pictures of models and pictures of actors to make a scene.

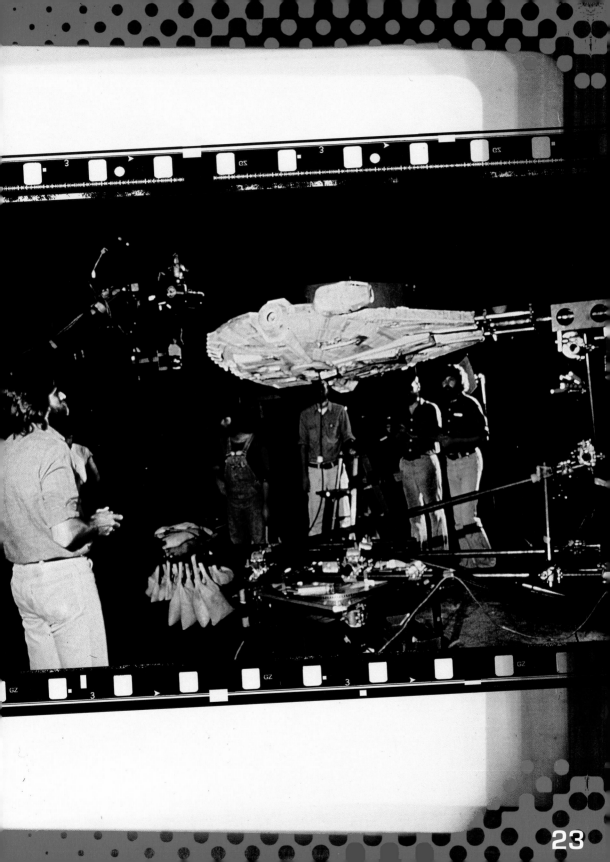

BRINGING PRETEND CHARACTERS TO LIFE

Motion capture makes animated characters move like people. Actors wear tight suits covered with tiny markers that reflect light. As actors move, cameras track the light reflected by the markers.

reflect—to bounce off an object

marker >>>

<<< marker

Computers collect marker data. On computers actors look like stick figures. Artists match the stick figures with points on characters' bodies. Matching the movements of actors and characters makes the characters seem to move like real people.

data—information or facts

Motion capture allowed Tom Hanks to play six characters in the 2004 movie *The Polar Express*.

MAKING SKIN LOOK REAL

Computers can give a made-up character's skin a warm glow for a more realistic look. Special effects created by computers can make almost anything seem real!

GLOSSARY

3-D (THREE-DEE)—having three dimensions: length, width, and depth

animate (AN-uh-mayt)—to make something appear to move

control (kuhn-TROHL)—a spot marked on an animated character where it can move

cyborg (SY-borg)—a human with robotic parts

data (DAY-tuh)—information or facts

frame (FRAYM)—one drawing or picture in a movie

freeze-action (FREEZ-AK-shuhn)—stopped while in motion

model (MOD-uhl)—something that is made to look like a person, animal, or object

reflect (ri-FLEKT)—to bounce off an object

special effect (SPESH-uhl uh-FEKT)—a misleading image created for movies by using makeup, special props, camera systems, computer graphics, and other methods

READ MORE

Craig, Jonathan, and Bridget Light. *Special Effects Make-up Artist.* The Coolest Jobs on the Planet. Chicago: Capstone Raintree, 2014.

Miles, Liz. *Movie Special Effects.* Culture in Action. Chicago: Raintree, 2010.

Mullins, Matt. *Special Effects Technician.* Cool Arts Careers. Ann Arbor, Mich.: Cherry Lake Pub., 2012.

INTERNET SITES

FactHound offers a safe, fun way to find Internet sites related to this book. All of the sites on FactHound have been researched by our staff.

Here's all you do:

Visit *www.facthound.com*

Type in this code: 9781491420010

 Check out projects, games and lots more at **www.capstonekids.com**

INDEX